Crock
the Kite

Written and Illustrated by

John Ryan

One day, Mr Noah decided to show his son Jaffet and Jaffet's friend Jannet all the birds on the Ark.

So they went up into the roof where the birds lived.

First of all they saw the very little birds like the robins, tits, wagtails, and wrens . . .

Then they saw the middle-sized birds like the ducks;

and the pheasants, the hens and the roosters.

They saw birds
with long legs and
long beaks and
birds with short legs
and short beaks;

beautiful birds like the peacock,

and ugly ones
like the vulture.

There were a lot of very funny-looking birds like penguins, pelicans and toucans.

There were sea birds like albatrosses, gulls and cormorants.

There were parrots who could talk just like people,

and there were ostriches who were so tall that the children couldn't reach high enough to measure them.

Last of all Mr Noah showed the children an eagle.

'He is the king of the birds,' said Mr Noah, 'the strongest and finest flier of them all. And now,' he went on, 'it's time you birds had some exercise. I'm going to let you out, but remember, none of you must go far from the Ark, and you must all come back again!'

Then Mr Noah opened a skylight in the roof of the Ark

and out flew the birds.

Round and round they flew, screeching and squawking, chirping and twittering, flapping and fluttering,

until they were all whirling in a great circle high above the Ark.

Down on the deck Jaffet and Jannet, Mrs Noah, gloomy Mr and Mrs Shem and happy Mr and Mrs Ham were all watching.

Quite a lot of the animals were watching too, and so were the birds who weren't much good at flying, and those who couldn't fly at all.

But there was one creature who wasn't watching the birds.

That was Crockle, the children's pet baby crocodile who shouldn't have been on the Ark at all because there were already two perfectly good (or bad) crocodiles on board. Crockle was behaving very oddly.

He was flapping his legs and jumping up and down,

higher and higher and harder and harder.

Then he climbed up on to a chair,

and jumped off it, waving his front legs wildly,

THUMP!

but he landed with a thump on his tummy!

'Poor Crockle,' said Jaffet. 'He's trying to fly like a bird!

'But it's no good, Crockle, people and animals *can't* fly.'

'But kites can,' said Ham, who had been listening, 'and that reminds me . . . .

Away he went and came back with a beautiful big kite which he had made specially for Jaffet and Jannet.

Then Ham showed the children how to fly the kite. By this time the birds had all come back to the deck of the Ark. They stood and watched. So did Crockle.

When the children understood what to do, Ham and the other grown-ups and some of the animals went indoors for their afternoon snooze. They left the children to play.

It was great fun. The wind was just right and Jannet and Jaffet took it in turns to hold the string.

Crockle watched. He seemed to be enjoying it every bit as much as the children.

Suddenly the wind dropped. The kite fluttered and the string fell loosely on the deck.

Then the wind blew harder again. The kite flew up, the string tightened and went up too . . .

. . . and with it went Crockle! The baby crocodile was hanging on to the string! He had been watching and waiting for his chance and now he had it!

He was flying at last. But the children knew it wasn't such a good idea. They didn't know whether to tell him to let go before he got too high, or to hang on because he already had so far to fall!

And the wind was getting stronger. 'Quick!' shouted Jaffet. 'Help me pull him down!' So Jannet caught hold of the string and they both tugged hard.

But then the wind gave a sudden, extra-strong gust . . .

. . . and the string snapped!

Crockle really was away now! Further and further, higher and higher above the Ark he soared.

At first he had thought flying was wonderful,

but now he was beginning to feel very far from home and also rather sick.

The kite threw him this way and that, and the Ark and the water seemed to turn first on one side and then on the other.

Sometimes it was even upside down! Crockle began to wish he had never even *thought* about flying.

Down below on the Ark, the two children were getting really frightened, Crockle was such a very long way away by now.

Then Jannet thought of something. She remembered what Mr Noah had said about eagles, how strong they were and how high they could fly. She went to one of them and pointed to the kite and Crockle clinging to the string far away above them. The eagle seemed to understand.

In a moment he had taken off.

A few seconds later he was high in the air.

Then quite suddenly he had the string in his strong beak,

and was starting to pull the kite *and* Crockle . . .

. . . down, down in a wide swooping circle

towards the Ark and the children and animals waiting anxiously below.

Very soon Crockle was lowered safely into the arms of Jaffet and Jannet.

They were so happy that they found it hard to be really cross with Crockle. Then the children thanked the eagle. He was quite friendly even if he did look rather fierce.

'And now,' said Jaffet, 'we'd better put the birds away, and take Crockle in before he gets into any more trouble!'

'Yes,' said Jannet. 'Just look at him with that parrot!'

'He'll be learning to *talk* next!'